BIG-NOTE PIANO

GREAT SONGS OF
RODGERS & HAMMERSTEIN

ISBN 978-1-4803-4425-9

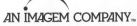

WILLIAMSON MUSIC®

AN IMAGEM COMPANY™
www.williamsonmusic.com

EXCLUSIVELY DISTRIBUTED BY

HAL•LEONARD®
CORPORATION
7777 W. BLUEMOUND RD. P.O. BOX 13819 MILWAUKEE, WI 53213

In Australia Contact:
Hal Leonard Australia Pty. Ltd.
4 Lentara Court
Cheltenham, Victoria, 3192 Australia
Email: ausadmin@halleonard.com.au

Visit Hal Leonard Online at
www.halleonard.com

T0057505

CONTENTS

BALI HA'I

from SOUTH PACIFIC

Lyrics by OSCAR HAMMERSTEIN II
Music by RICHARD RODGERS

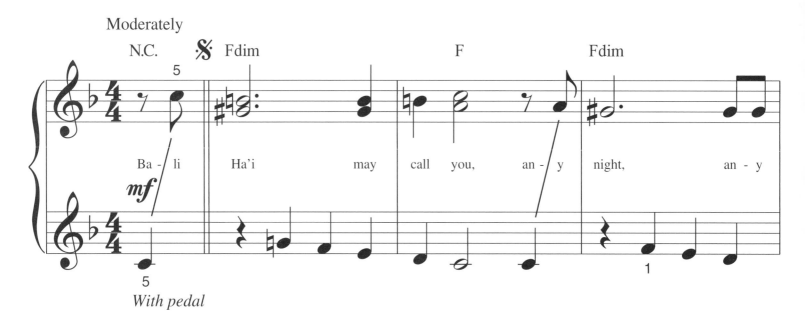

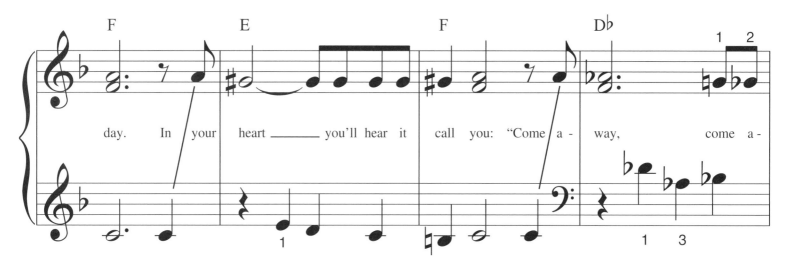

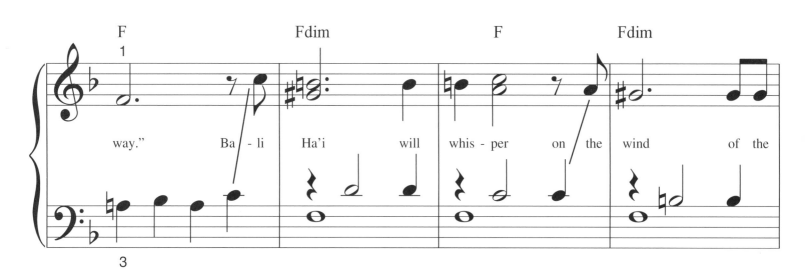

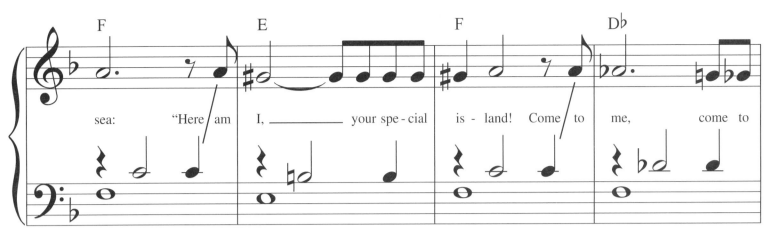

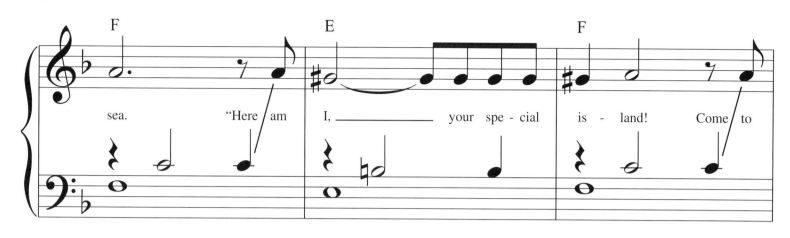

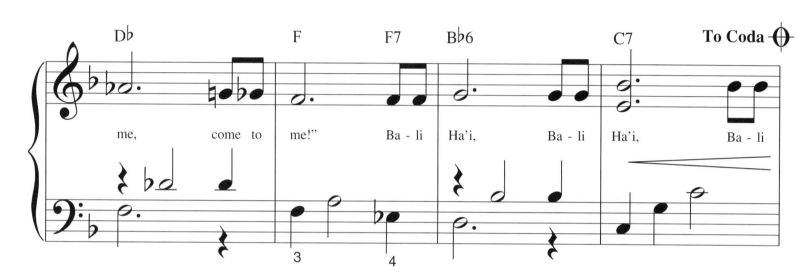

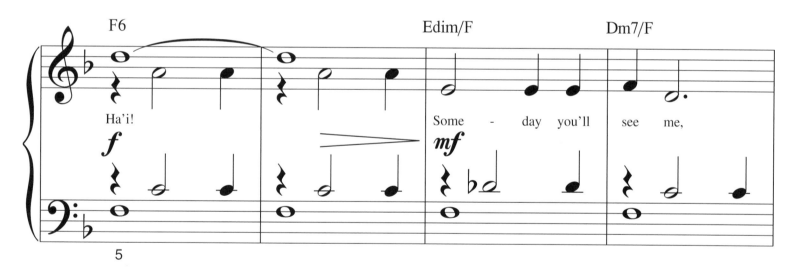

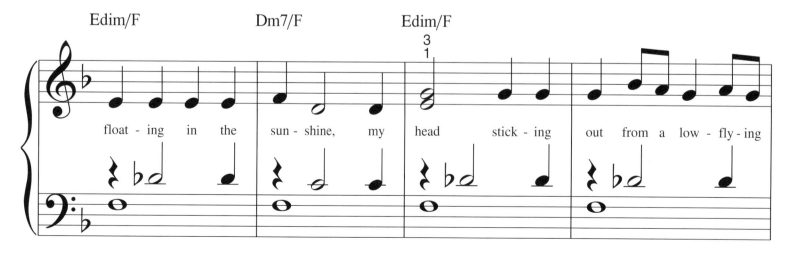

cloud. _____ You'll hear me call you,

sing - ing through the sun - shine, sweet and clear as can

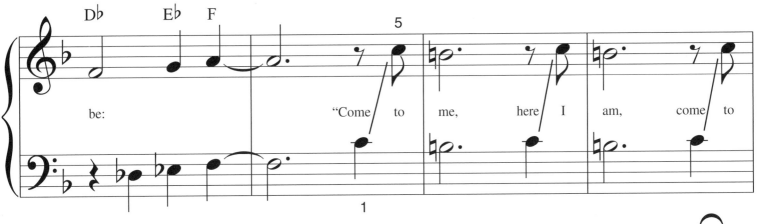

be: "Come to me, here I am, come to

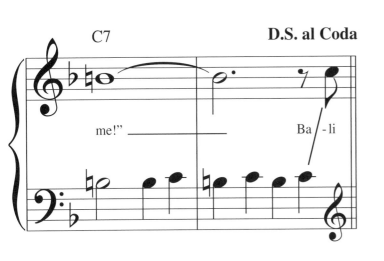

D.S. al Coda

me!" _____ Ba - li

CODA

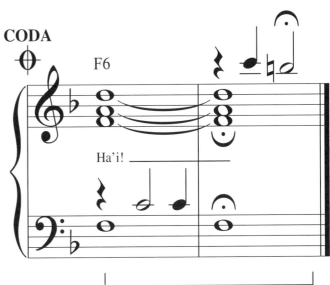

Ha'i! _____

CLIMB EV'RY MOUNTAIN
from THE SOUND OF MUSIC

Lyrics by OSCAR HAMMERSTEIN II
Music by RICHARD RODGERS

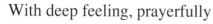

With deep feeling, prayerfully

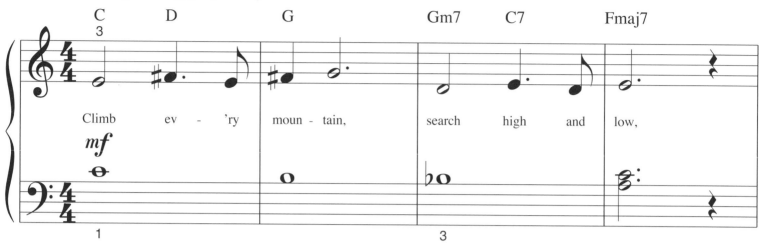

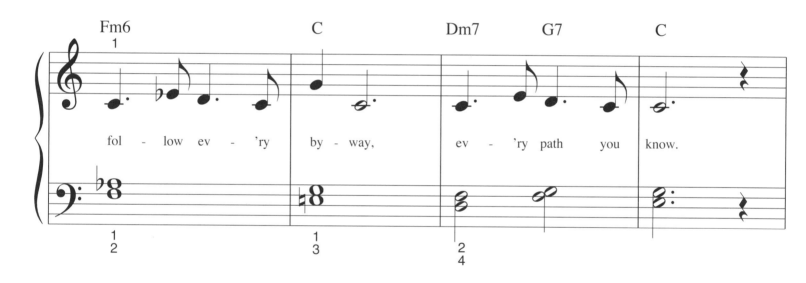

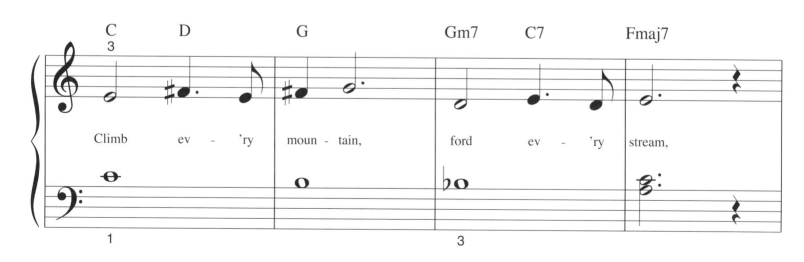

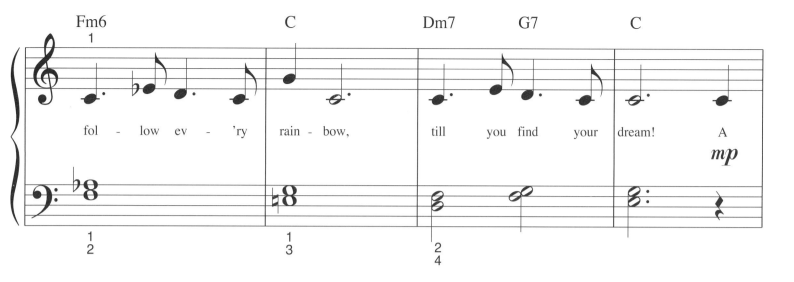

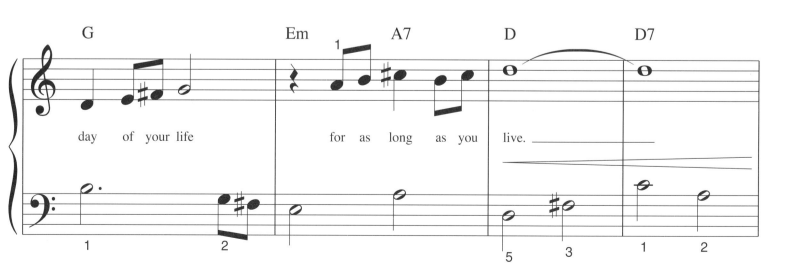

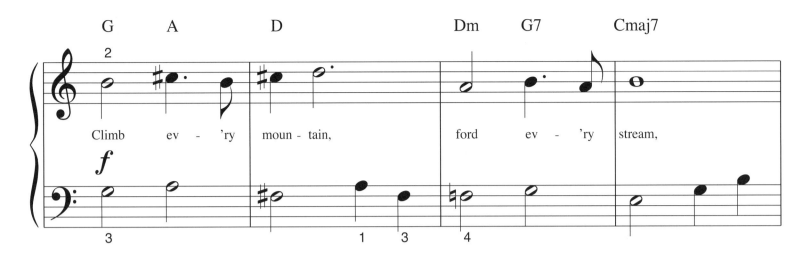

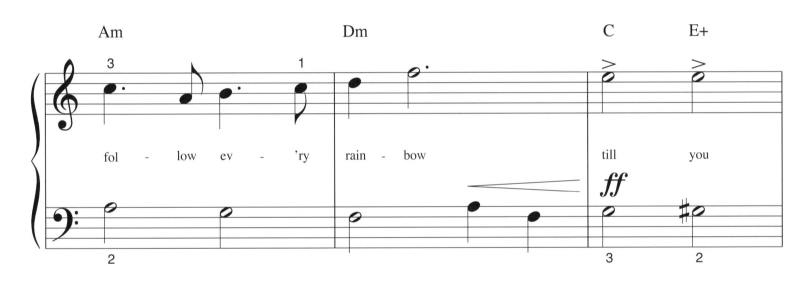

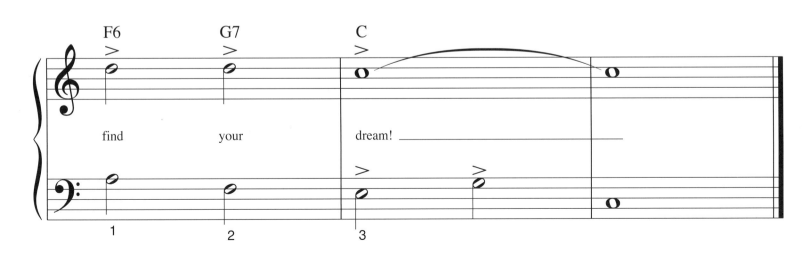

DO I LOVE YOU
BECAUSE YOU'RE BEAUTIFUL?
from CINDERELLA

Lyrics by OSCAR HAMMERSTEIN II
Music by RICHARD RODGERS

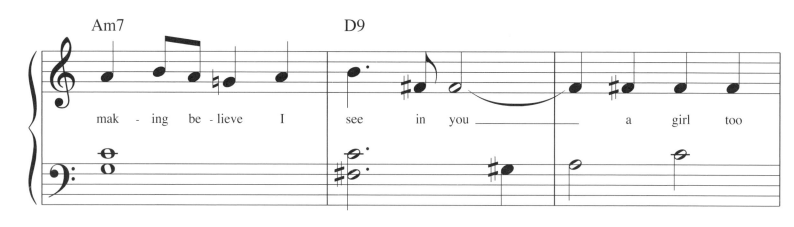

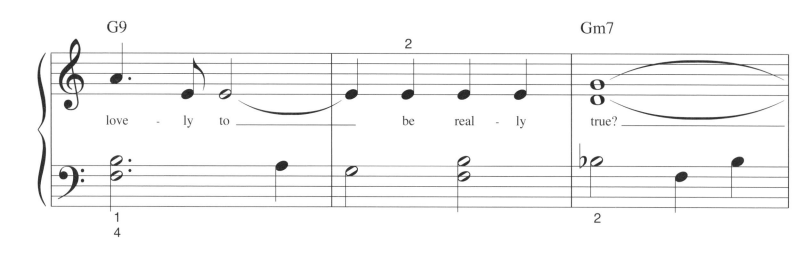

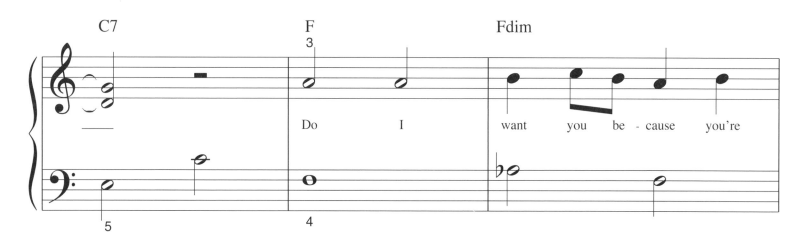

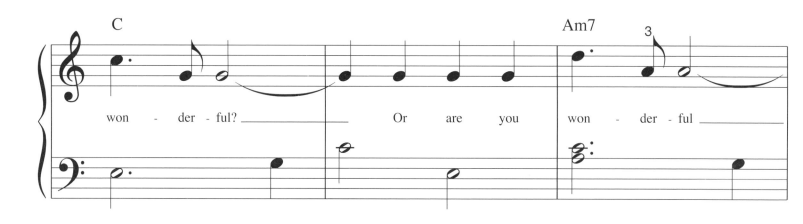

DO-RE-MI

from THE SOUND OF MUSIC

Lyrics by OSCAR HAMMERSTEIN II
Music by RICHARD RODGERS

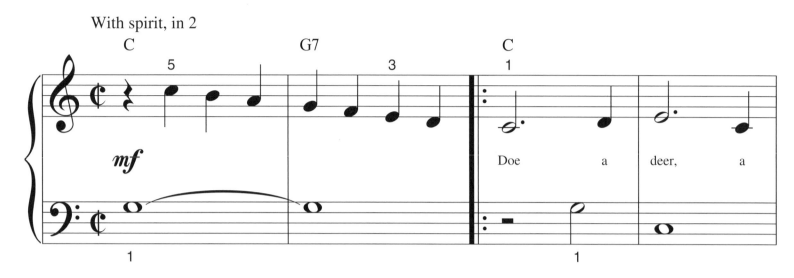

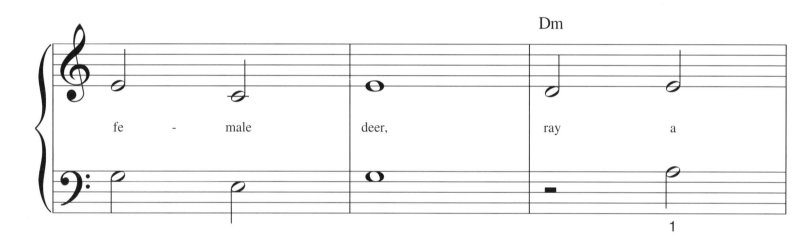

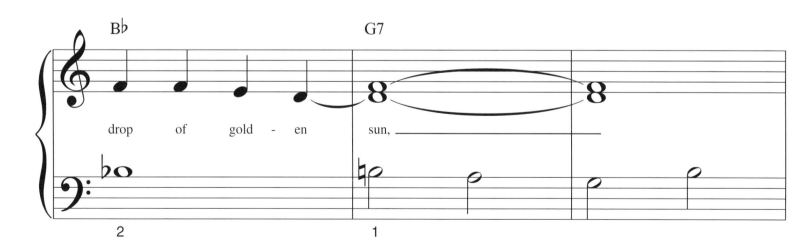

I HAVE DREAMED
from THE KING AND I

Lyrics by OSCAR HAMMERSTEIN II
Music by RICHARD RODGERS

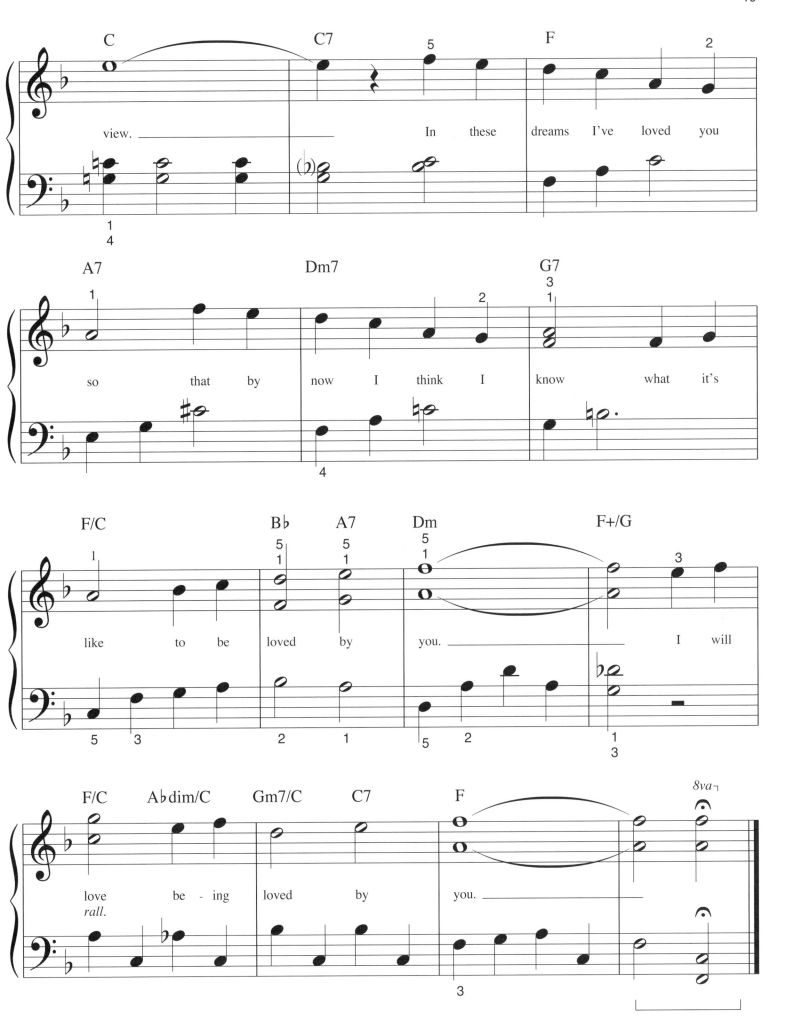

EDELWEISS
from THE SOUND OF MUSIC

Lyrics by OSCAR HAMMERSTEIN II
Music by RICHARD RODGERS

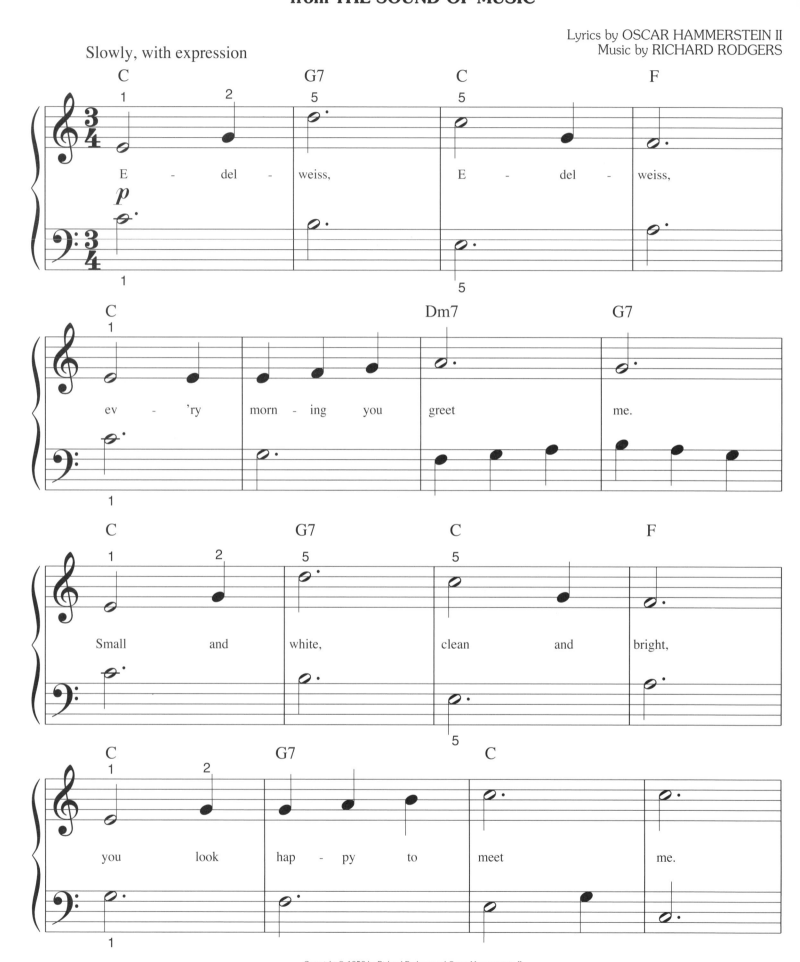

HELLO, YOUNG LOVERS
from THE KING AND I

Lyrics by OSCAR HAMMERSTEIN II
Music by RICHARD RODGERS

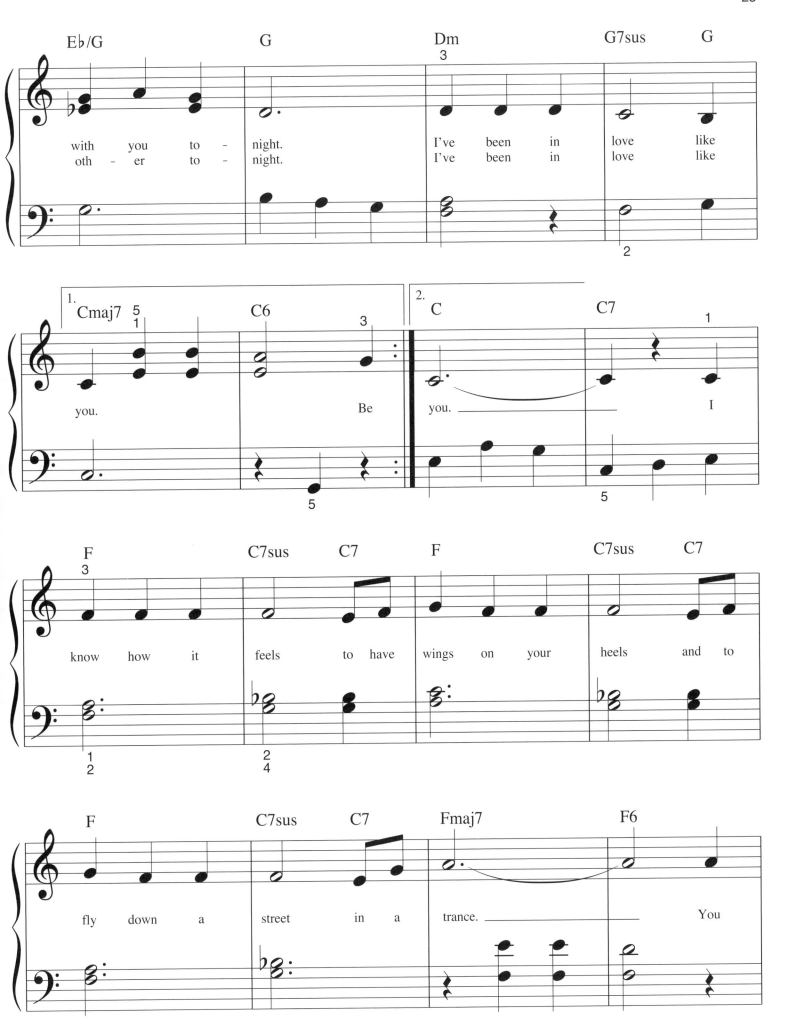

HONEY BUN
from SOUTH PACIFIC

Lyrics by OSCAR HAMMERSTEIN II
Music by RICHARD RODGERS

I WHISTLE A HAPPY TUNE

from THE KING AND I

Lyrics by OSCAR HAMMERSTEIN II
Music by RICHARD RODGERS

Moderately, in 2

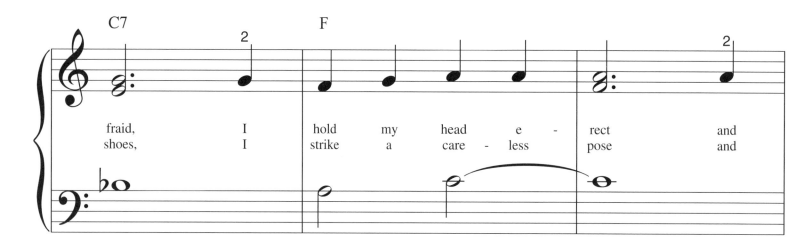

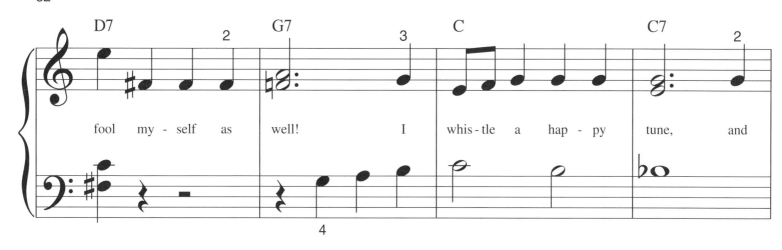

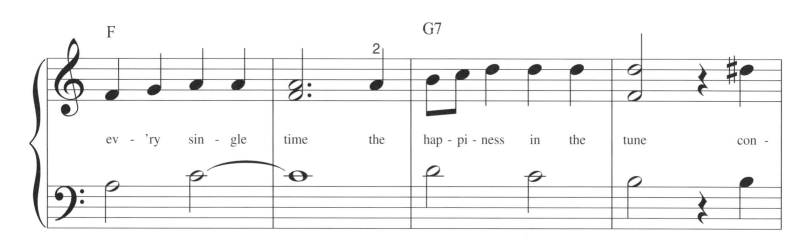

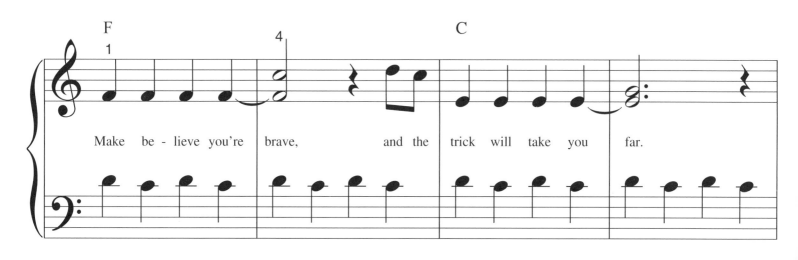

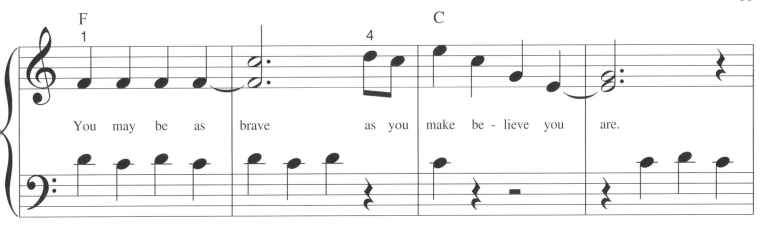

You may be as brave as you make be-lieve you are.

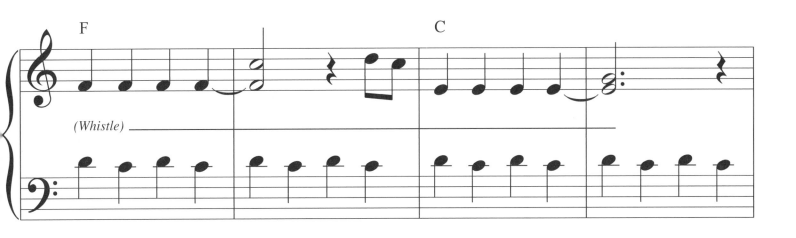

(Whistle)

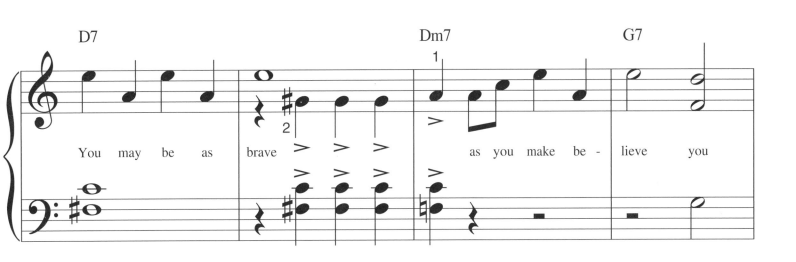

You may be as brave as you make be-lieve you

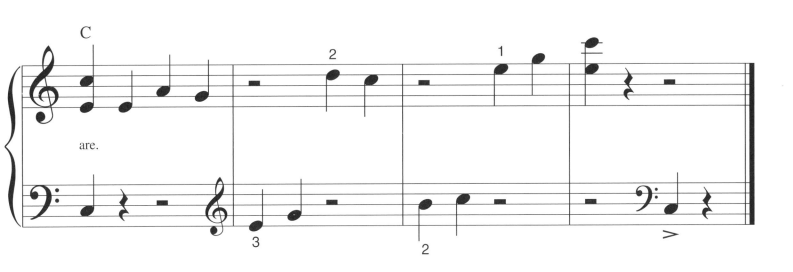

are.

IF I LOVED YOU
from CAROUSEL

Lyrics by OSCAR HAMMERSTEIN II
Music by RICHARD RODGERS

IT MIGHT AS WELL BE SPRING

from STATE FAIR

Lyrics by OSCAR HAMMERSTEIN II
Music by RICHARD RODGERS

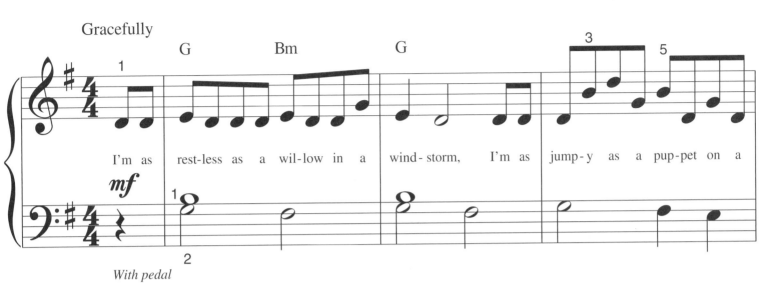

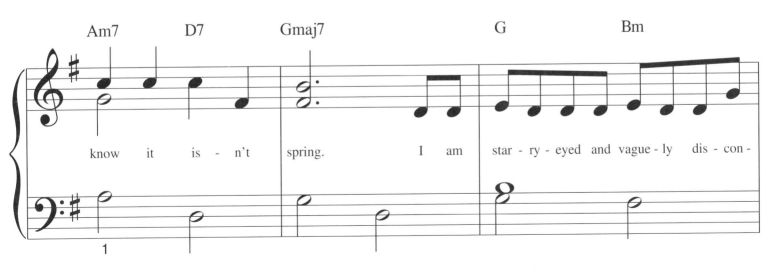

IT'S A GRAND NIGHT FOR SINGING

from STATE FAIR

Lyrics by OSCAR HAMMERSTEIN II
Music by RICHARD RODGERS

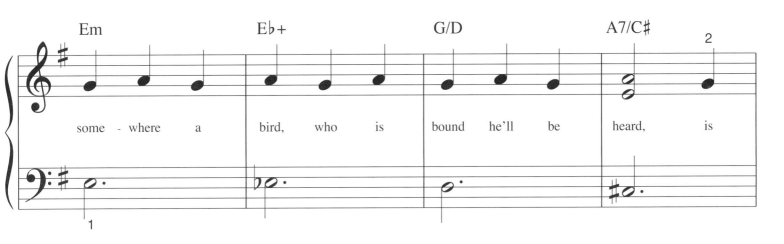

some - where a bird, who is bound he'll be heard, is

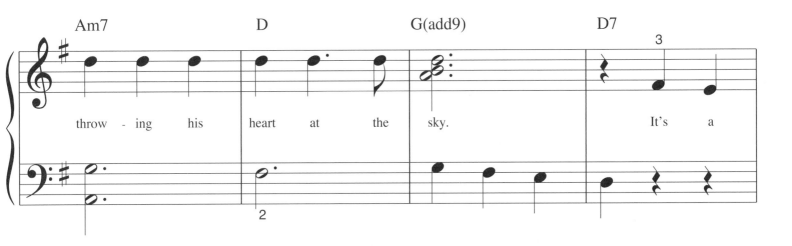

throw - ing his heart at the sky. It's a

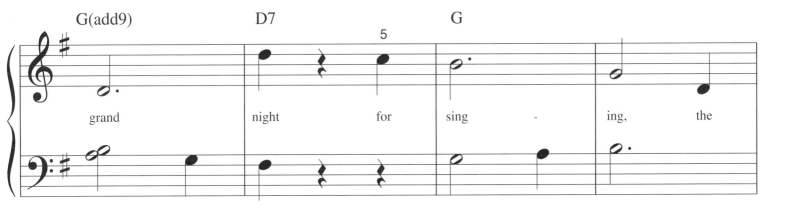

grand night for sing - ing, the

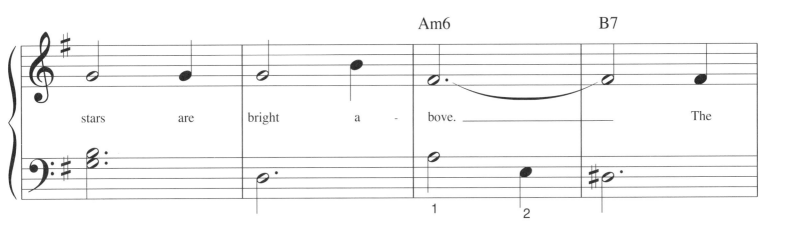

stars are bright a - bove. _____ The

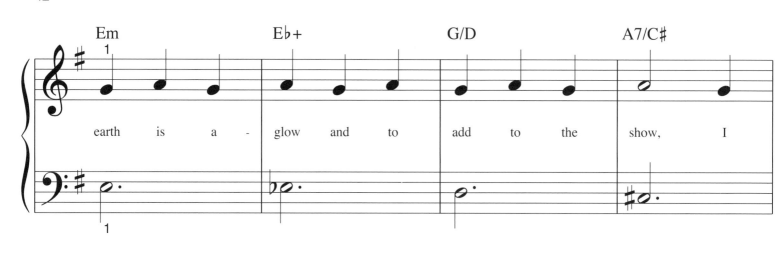

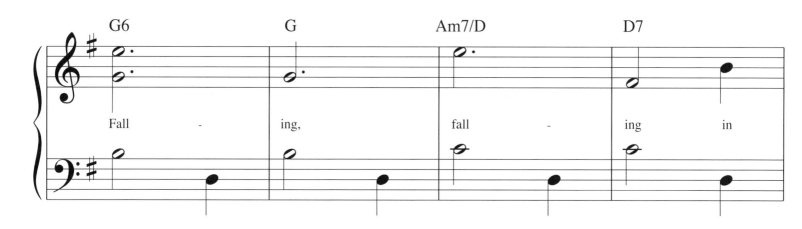

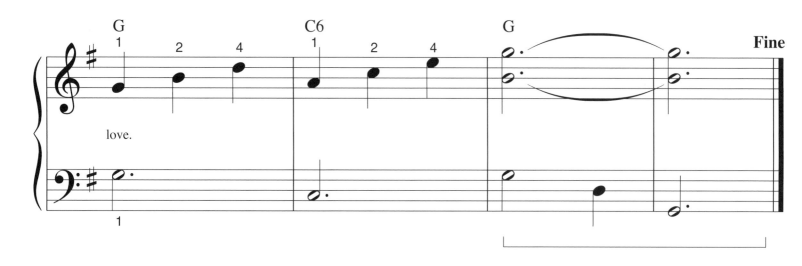

Interlude

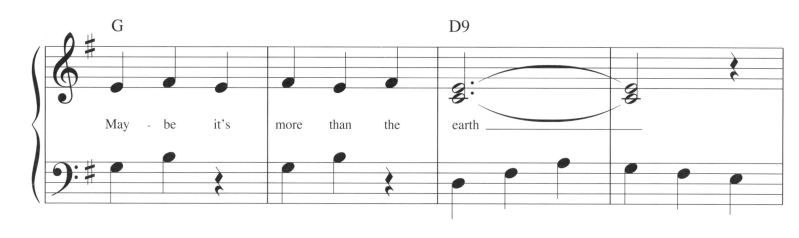

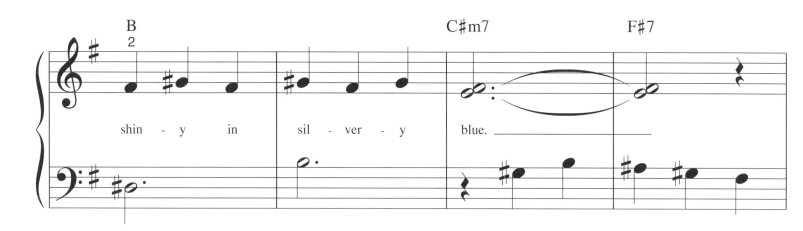

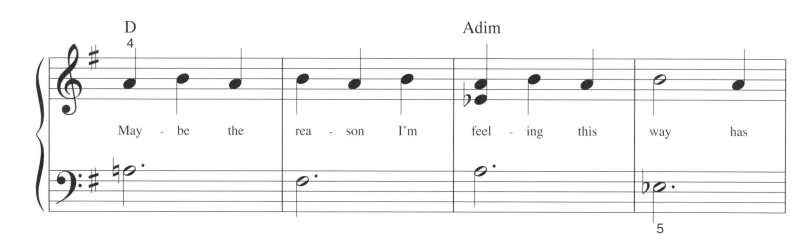

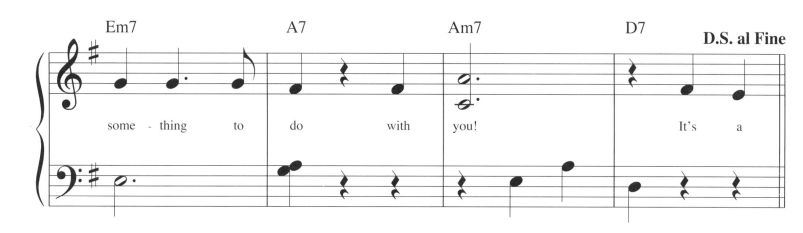

LOVE, LOOK AWAY

from FLOWER DRUM SONG

Lyrics by OSCAR HAMMERSTEIN II
Music by RICHARD RODGERS

JUNE IS BUSTIN' OUT ALL OVER

from CAROUSEL

Lyrics by OSCAR HAMMERSTEIN II
Music by RICHARD RODGERS

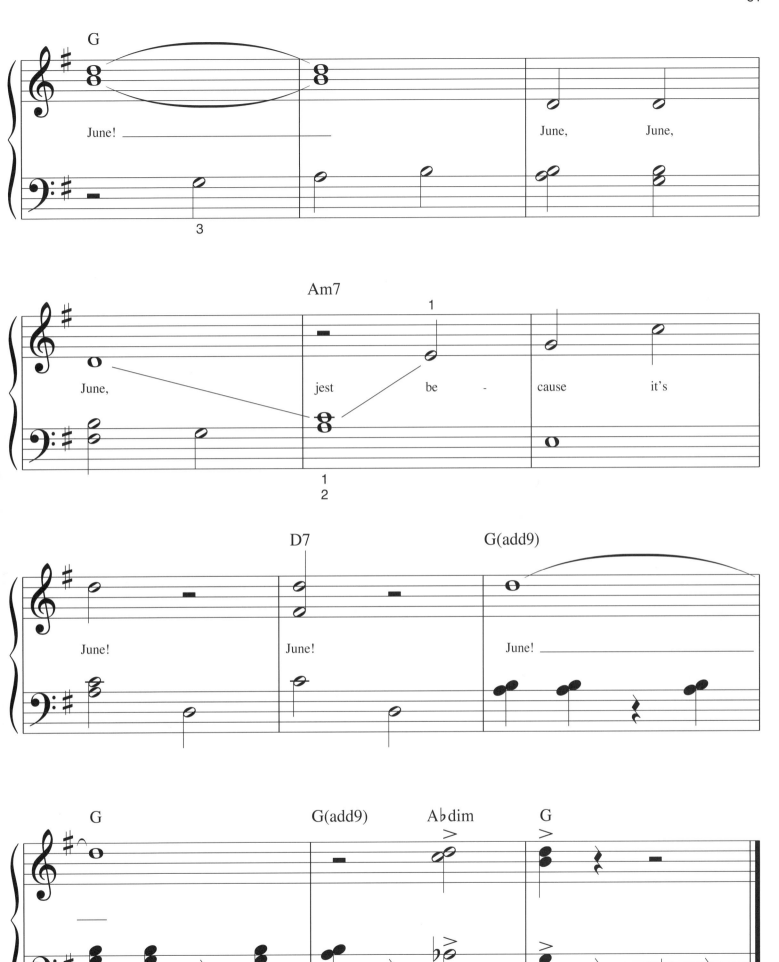

MARIA
from THE SOUND OF MUSIC

Lyrics by OSCAR HAMMERSTEIN II
Music by RICHARD RODGERS

54

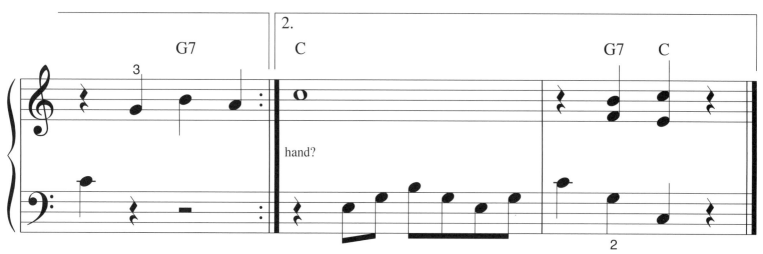

NO OTHER LOVE

from ME AND JULIET

Lyrics by OSCAR HAMMERSTEIN II
Music by RICHARD RODGERS

No oth - er love have I, __ on - ly my love for you, __ on - ly the dream we knew, __ no oth - er love. __ Watch - ing the night go by, __

MY FAVORITE THINGS
from THE SOUND OF MUSIC

Lyrics by OSCAR HAMMERSTEIN II
Music by RICHARD RODGERS

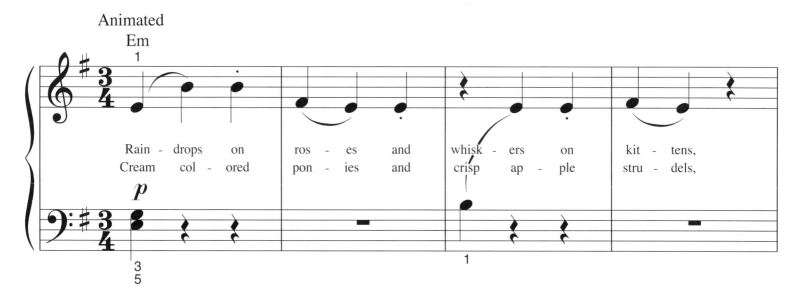

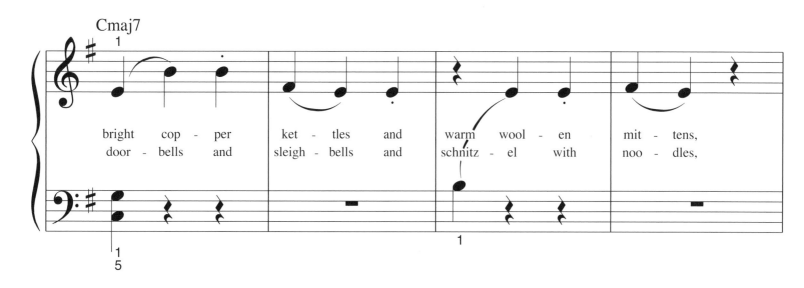

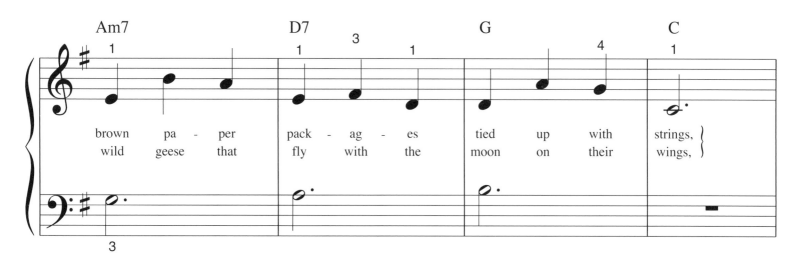

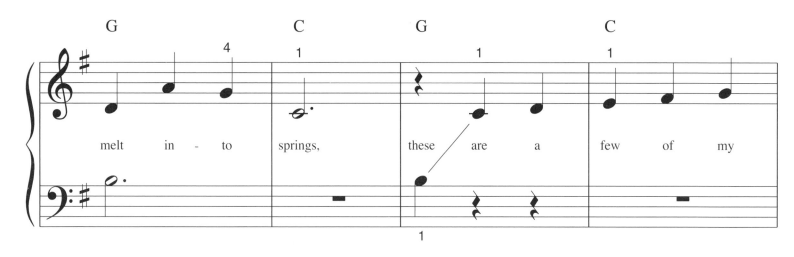

G   C   G   C

melt   in - to   springs,   these   are   a   few   of   my

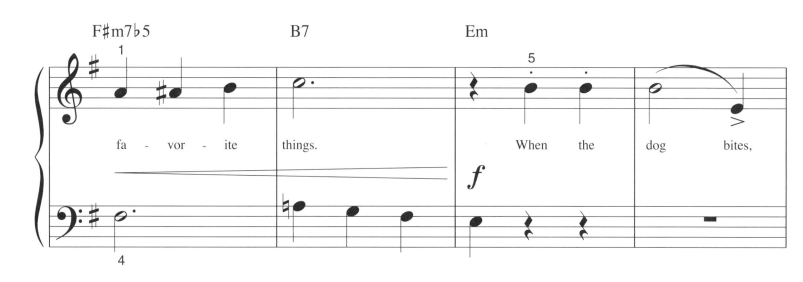

F♯m7♭5   B7   Em

fa - vor - ite   things.   When   the   dog   bites,

f

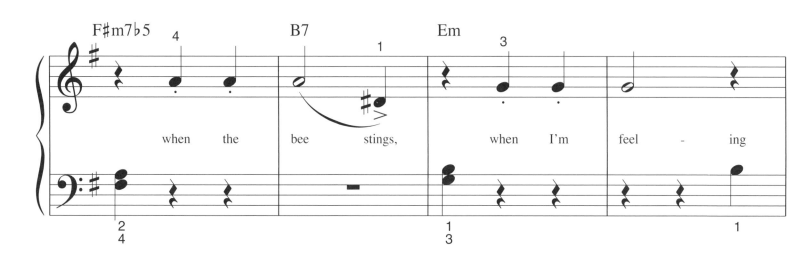

F♯m7♭5   B7   Em

when   the   bee   stings,   when   I'm   feel - ing

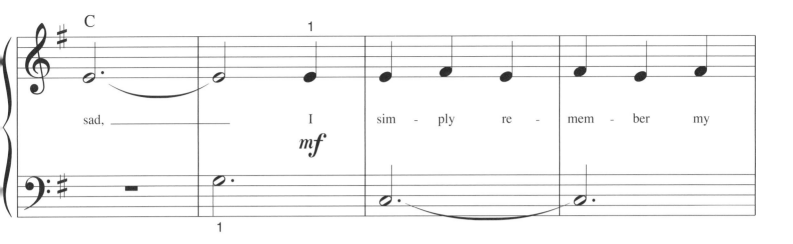

sad, _____ I sim - ply re - mem - ber my

mf

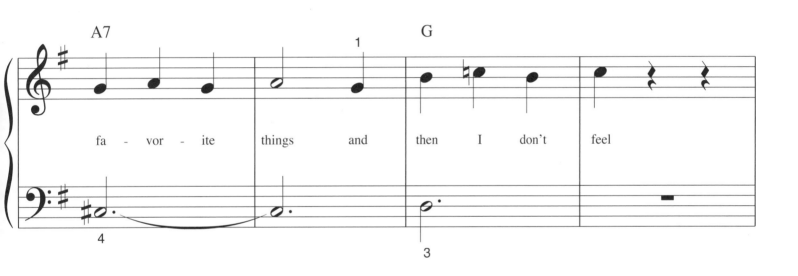

fa - vor - ite things and then I don't feel

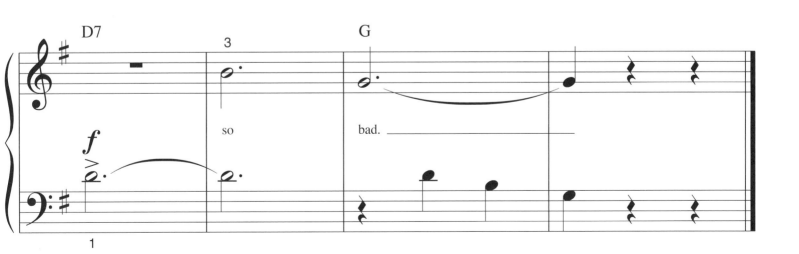

so bad. _____

f

OH, WHAT A BEAUTIFUL MORNIN'

from OKLAHOMA!

Lyrics by OSCAR HAMMERSTEIN II
Music by RICHARD RODGERS

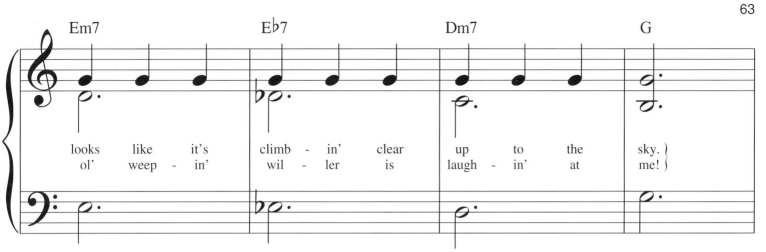

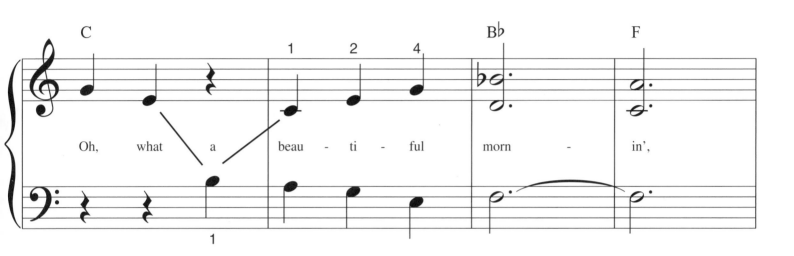

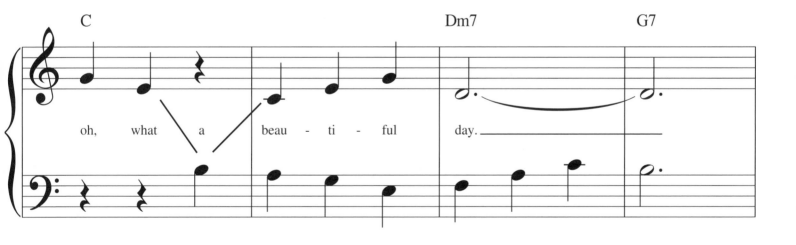

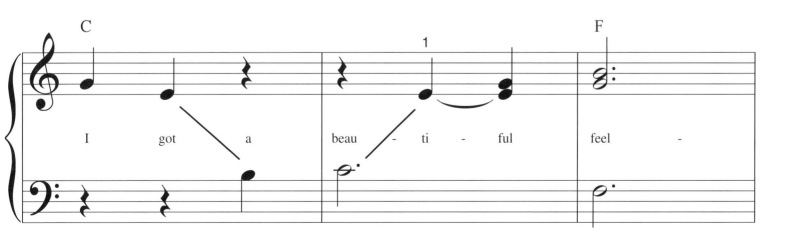

OKLAHOMA
from OKLAHOMA!

Lyrics by OSCAR HAMMERSTEIN II
Music by RICHARD RODGERS

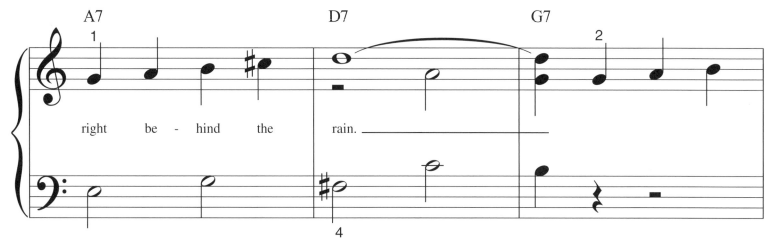

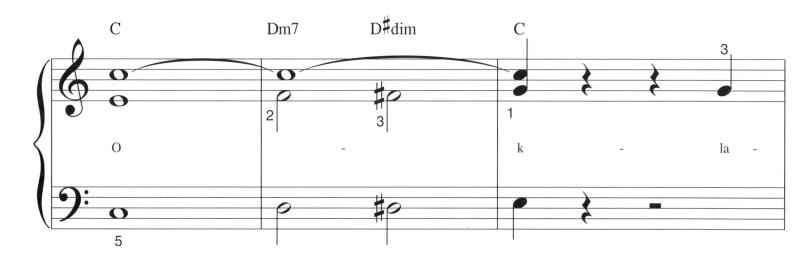

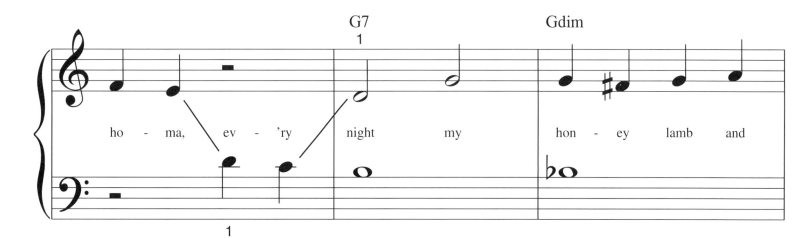

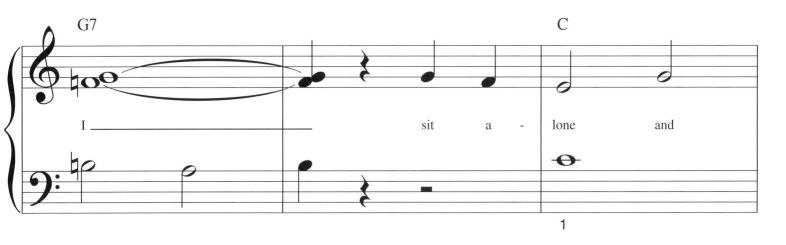

I _____ sit a - lone and

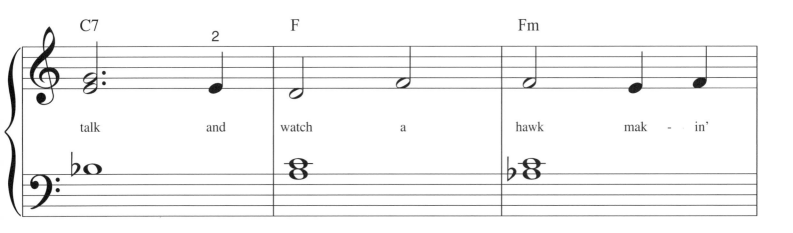

talk and watch a hawk mak - in'

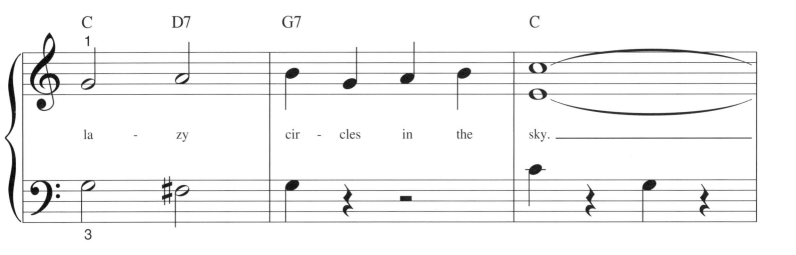

la - zy cir - cles in the sky. _____

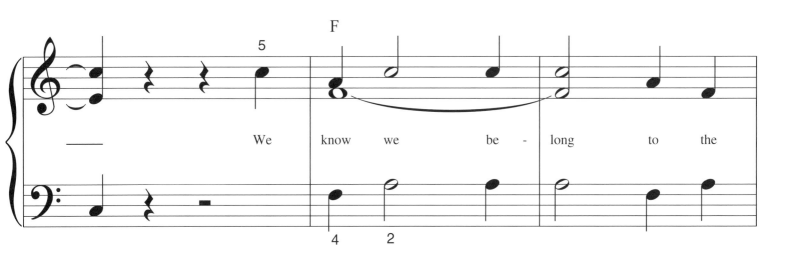

We know we be - long to the

land, _____ and the land we be -

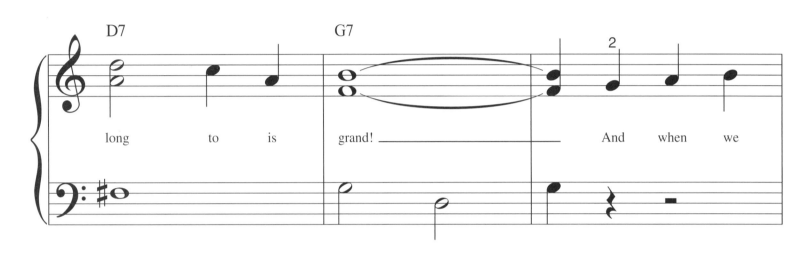

long to is grand! _____ And when we

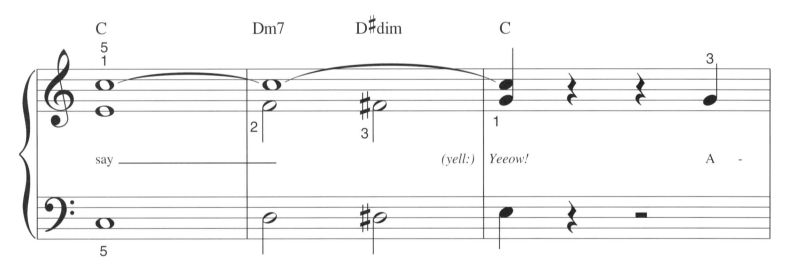

say _____ (yell:) *Yeeow!* A -

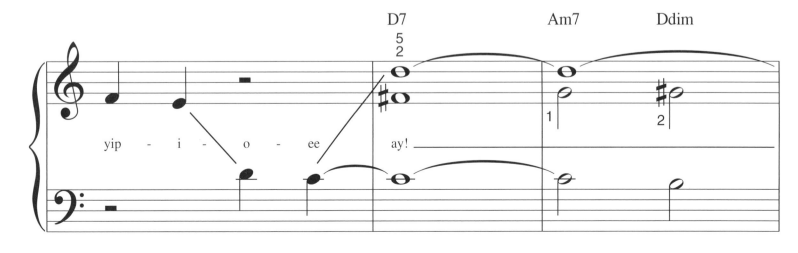

yip - i - o - ee ay! _____

PEOPLE WILL SAY WE'RE IN LOVE
from OKLAHOMA!

Lyrics by OSCAR HAMMERSTEIN II
Music by RICHARD RODGERS

C   D7

Don't   laugh   at   my   jokes   too   much.
Don't   stand   in   the   rain   with   me.

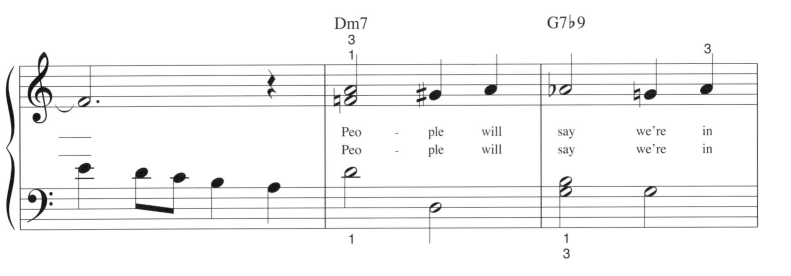

                        Dm7   G7♭9

Peo - ple   will   say   we're   in
Peo - ple   will   say   we're   in

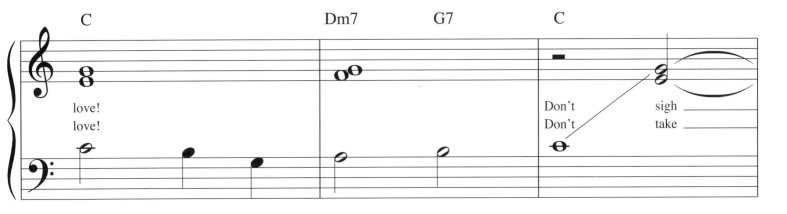

C   Dm7   G7   C

love!   Don't   sigh
love!   Don't   take

                        and   gaze   at   me.
                        my   arm   too   much.

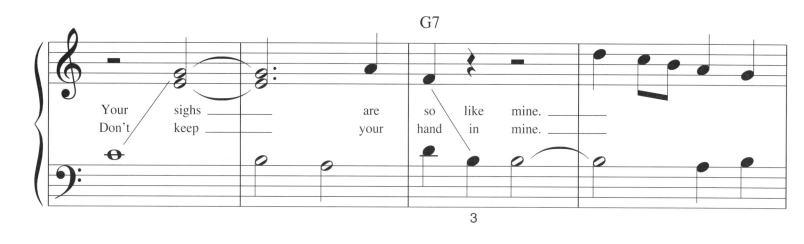

Your sighs ____ are so like mine. ____
Don't keep ____ your hand in mine. ____

Your eyes ____ must - n't glow like mine. ____
Your hand ____ feels so grand in mine. ____

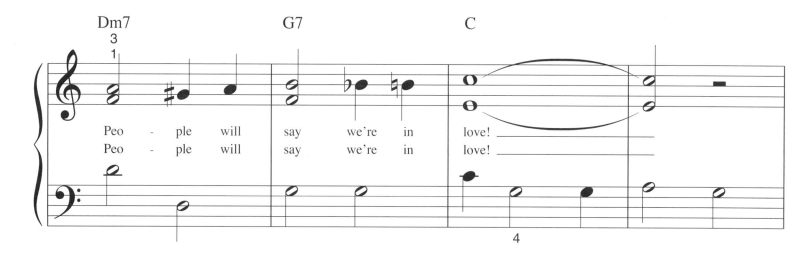

Peo - ple will say we're in love! ____
Peo - ple will say we're in love! ____

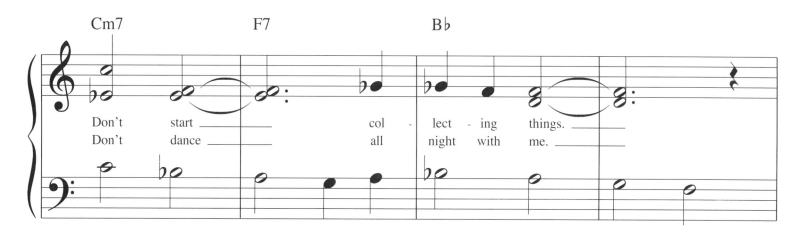

Don't start ____ col - lect - ing things. ____
Don't dance ____ all night with me. ____

SHALL WE DANCE?

from THE KING AND I

Lyrics by OSCAR HAMMERSTEIN II
Music by RICHARD RODGERS

Moderately, in 2

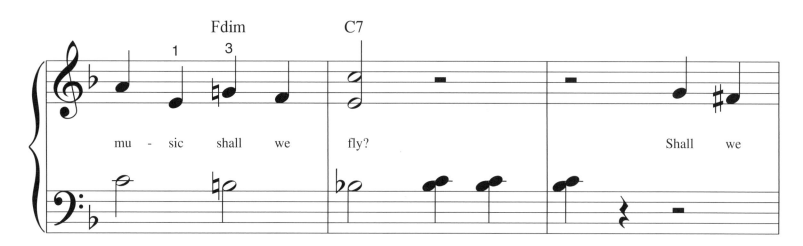

dance?　　　　　　　　　　　　　　Shall　we　then　say　"good -

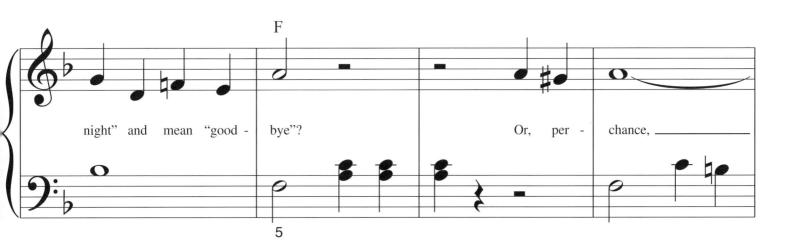

night" and mean "good - | bye"?　　　　　　Or, per - chance, _____

F

5

_____ when the | last | lit - tle | star has left the | sky,

Fdim　　Bb6　　Gm7

2

shall we | still be to - | geth - er with our | arms a - round each

C7　　　　　　　　　　　　　　F

3

2　　　　　　　　　3

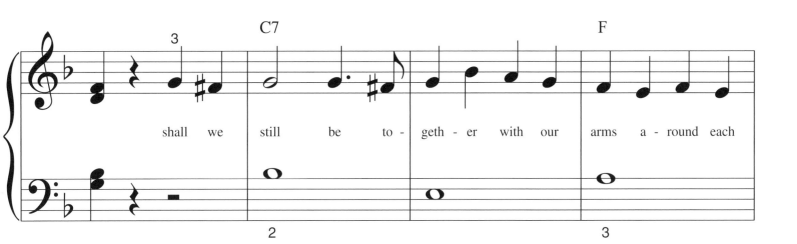

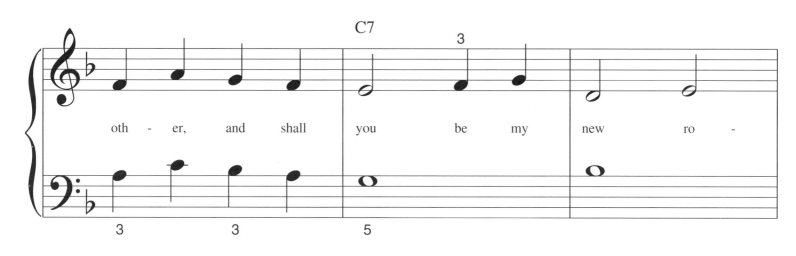

oth - er, and shall you be my new ro -

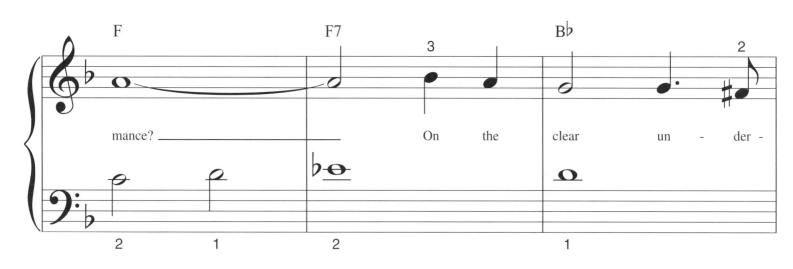

mance? _____ On the clear un - der -

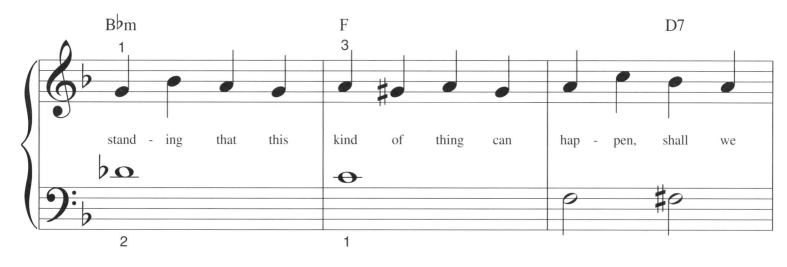

stand - ing that this kind of thing can hap - pen, shall we

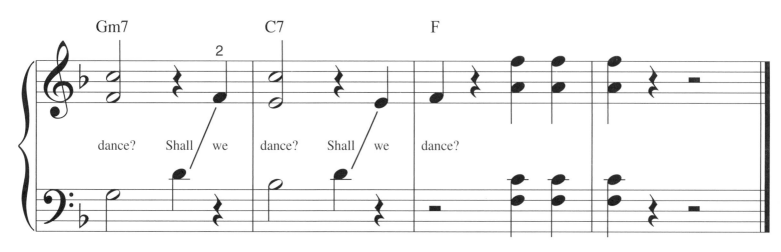

dance? Shall we dance? Shall we dance?

SOME ENCHANTED EVENING

from SOUTH PACIFIC

Lyrics by OSCAR HAMMERSTEIN II
Music by RICHARD RODGERS

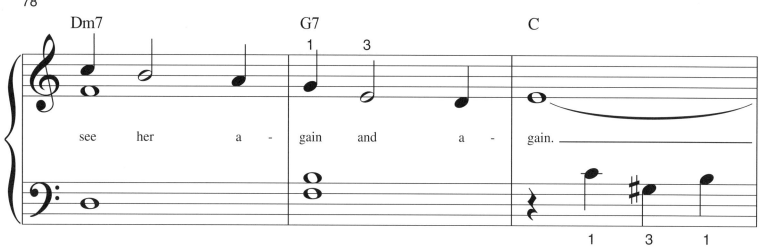

see her a - gain and a - gain.

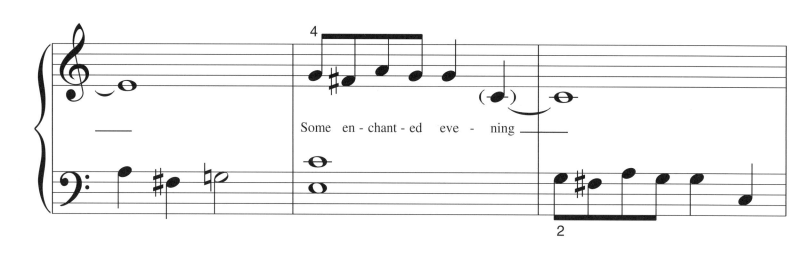

Some en - chant - ed eve - ning

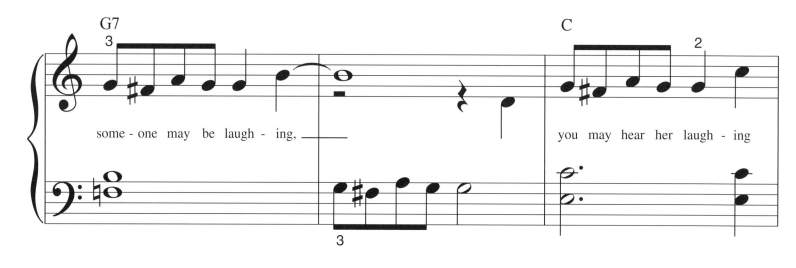

some - one may be laugh - ing, you may hear her laugh - ing

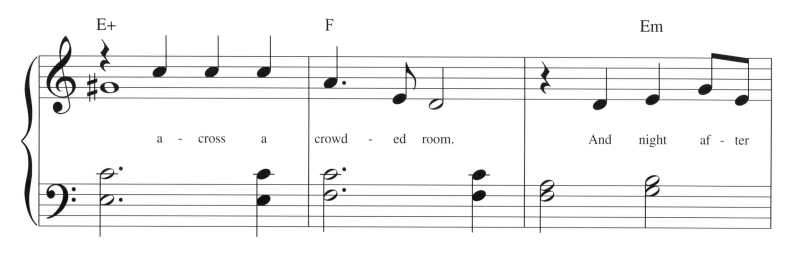

a - cross a crowd - ed room. And night af - ter

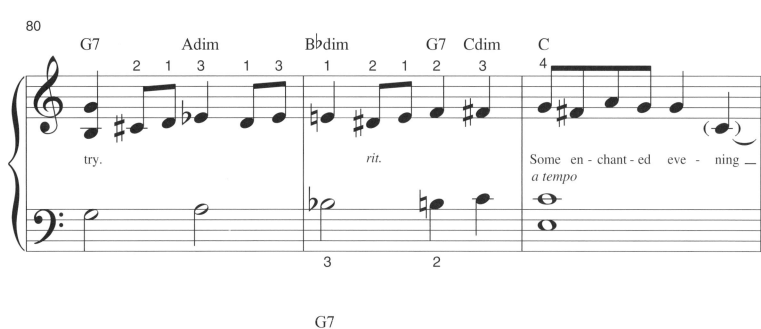

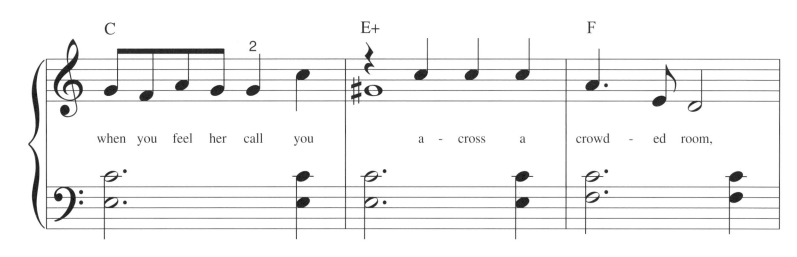

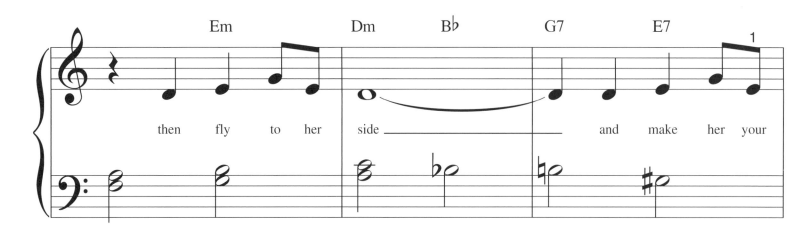

SOMETHING WONDERFUL

from THE KING AND I

Lyrics by OSCAR HAMMERSTEIN II
Music by RICHARD RODGERS

THE SOUND OF MUSIC
from THE SOUND OF MUSIC

Lyrics by OSCAR HAMMERSTEIN II
Music by RICHARD RODGERS

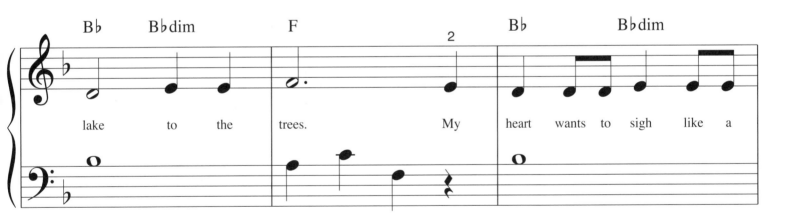

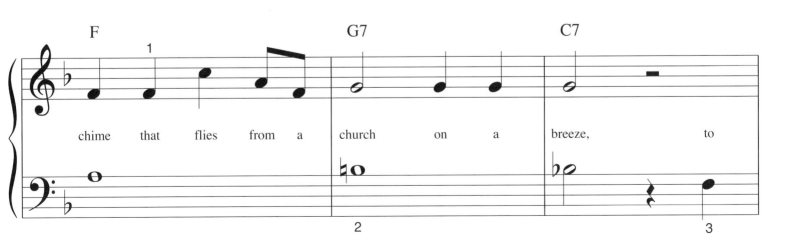

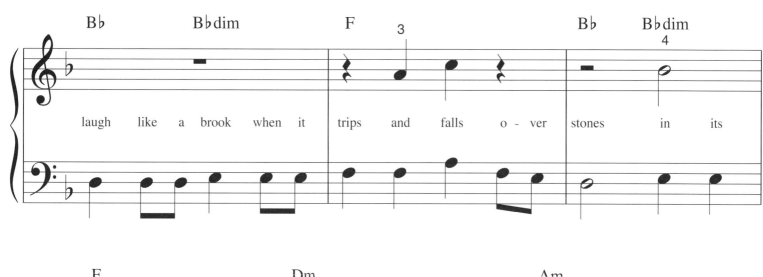

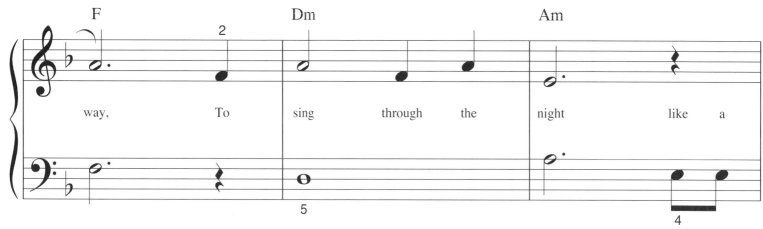

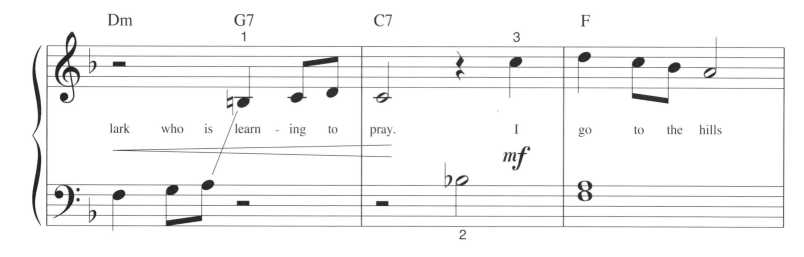

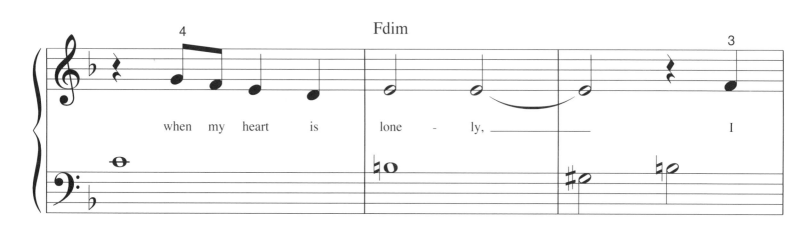

THE SURREY WITH THE FRINGE ON TOP

from OKLAHOMA!

Lyrics by OSCAR HAMMERSTEIN II
Music by RICHARD RODGERS

Moderately bright, in 2

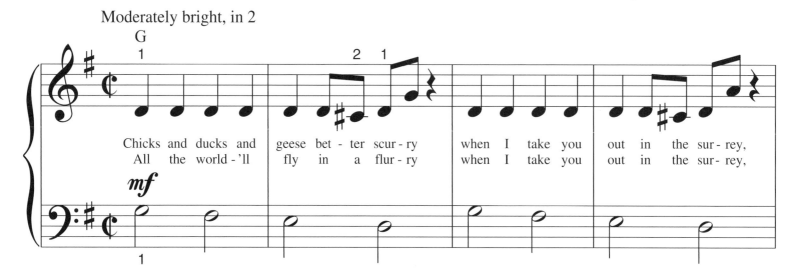

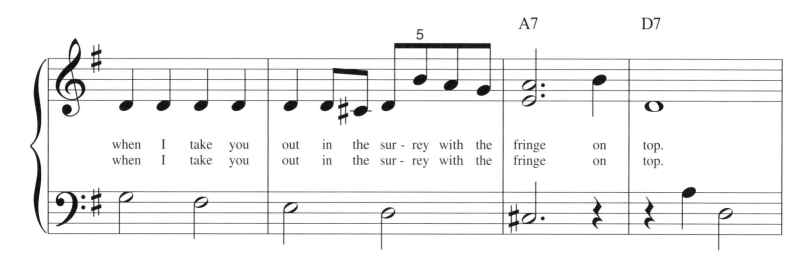

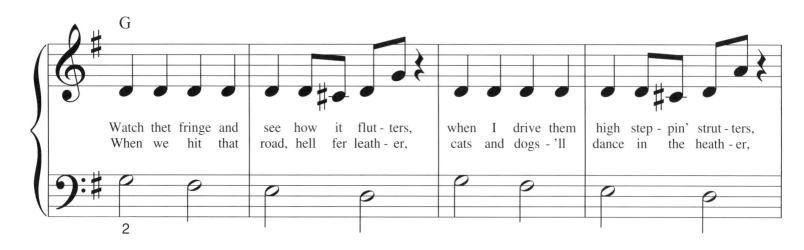

TEN MINUTES AGO
from CINDERELLA

Lyrics by OSCAR HAMMERSTEIN II
Music by RICHARD RODGERS

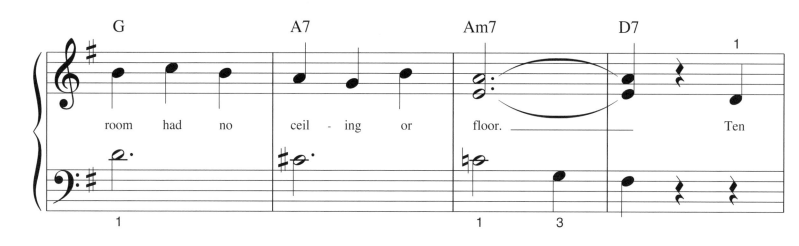

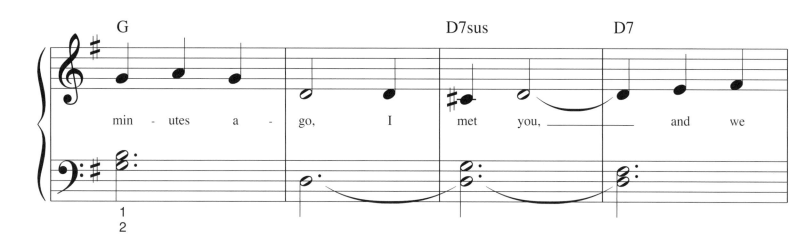

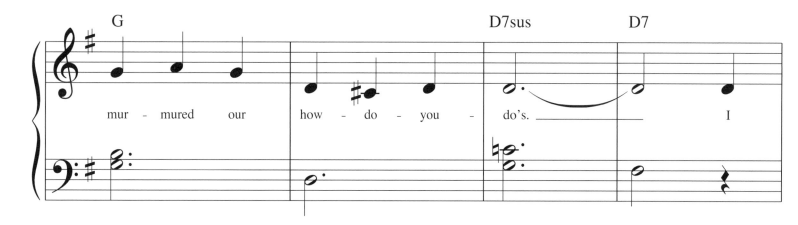

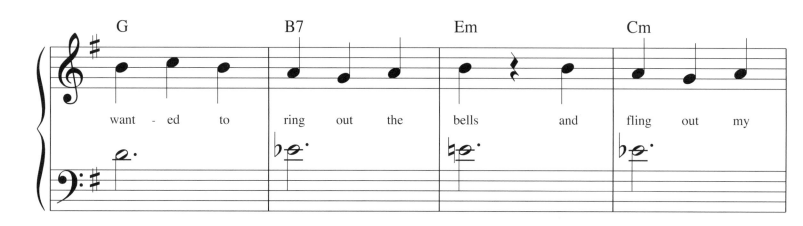

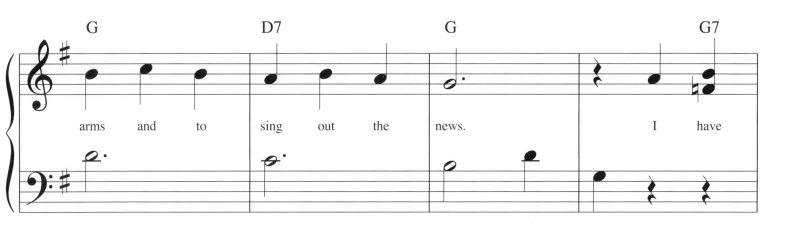

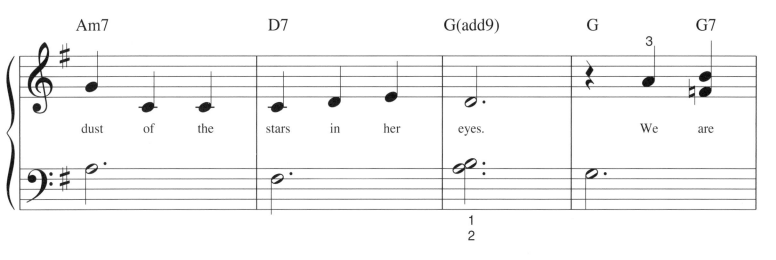

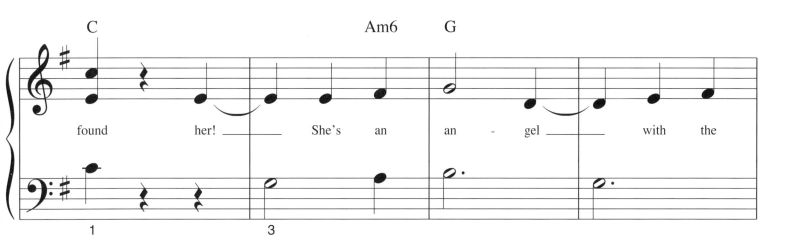

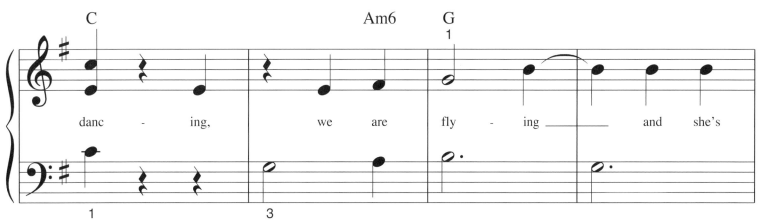

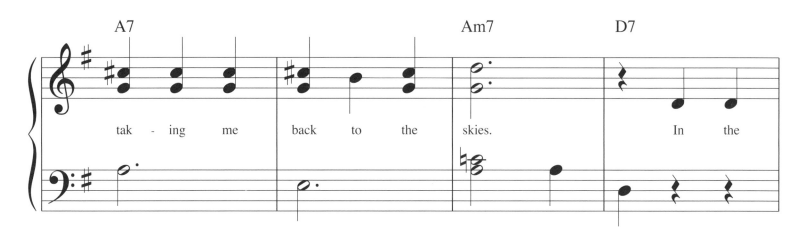

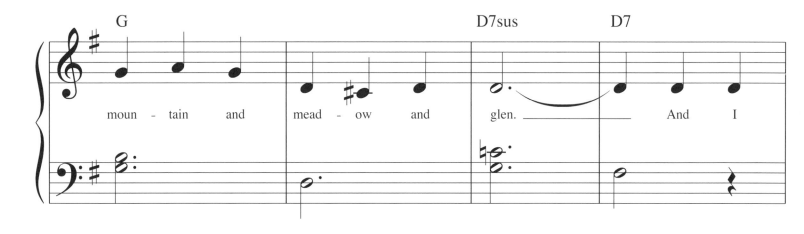

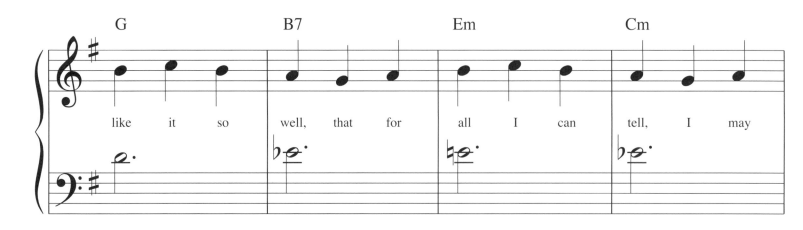

THERE IS NOTHIN' LIKE A DAME

from SOUTH PACIFIC

Lyrics by OSCAR HAMMERSTEIN II
Music by RICHARD RODGERS

We got

sun - light on the sand. We got moon - light on the sea. We got

man - goes and ba - na - nas you can pick right off a tree. We got

vol - ley - ball and ping - pong, and a lot of dan - dy games!

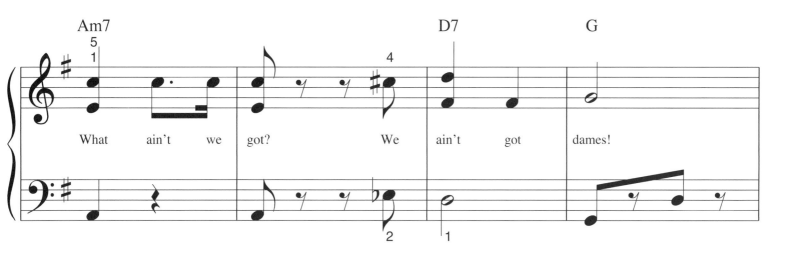

What ain't we got? We ain't got dames!

We get pack - ag - es from
rest - less, we feel

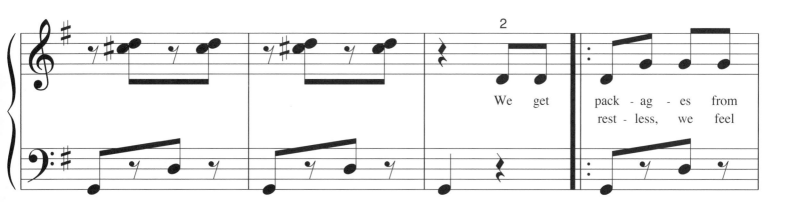

home. We get mov - ies, we get shows. We get speech - es from our
blue, we feel lone - ly and, in brief, we feel ev - 'ry kind of

skip - per, and ad - vice from Tok - yo Rose. We get let - ters doused with
feel - ing but the feel - ing of re - lief. We feel hun - gry as the

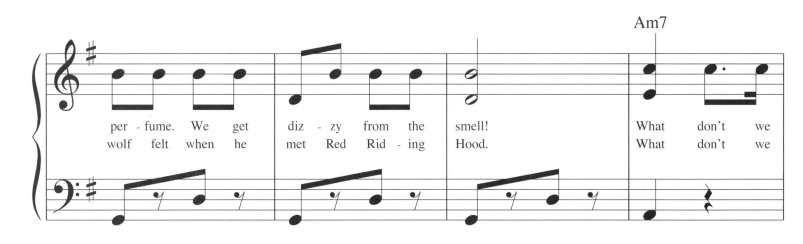

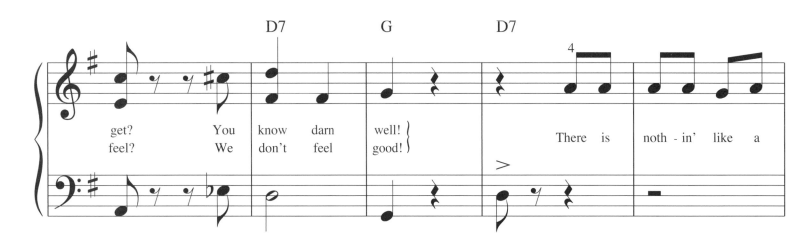

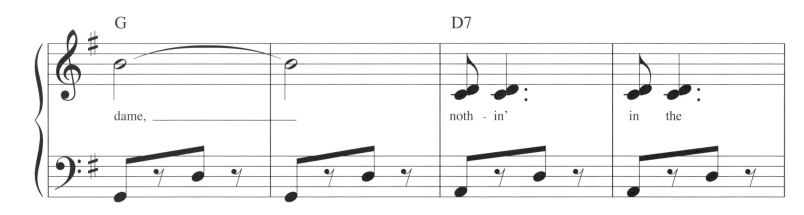

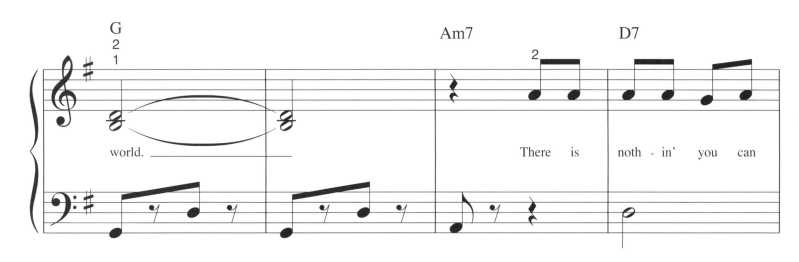

YOU ARE BEAUTIFUL
from FLOWER DRUM SONG

Lyrics by OSCAR HAMMERSTEIN II
Music by RICHARD RODGERS

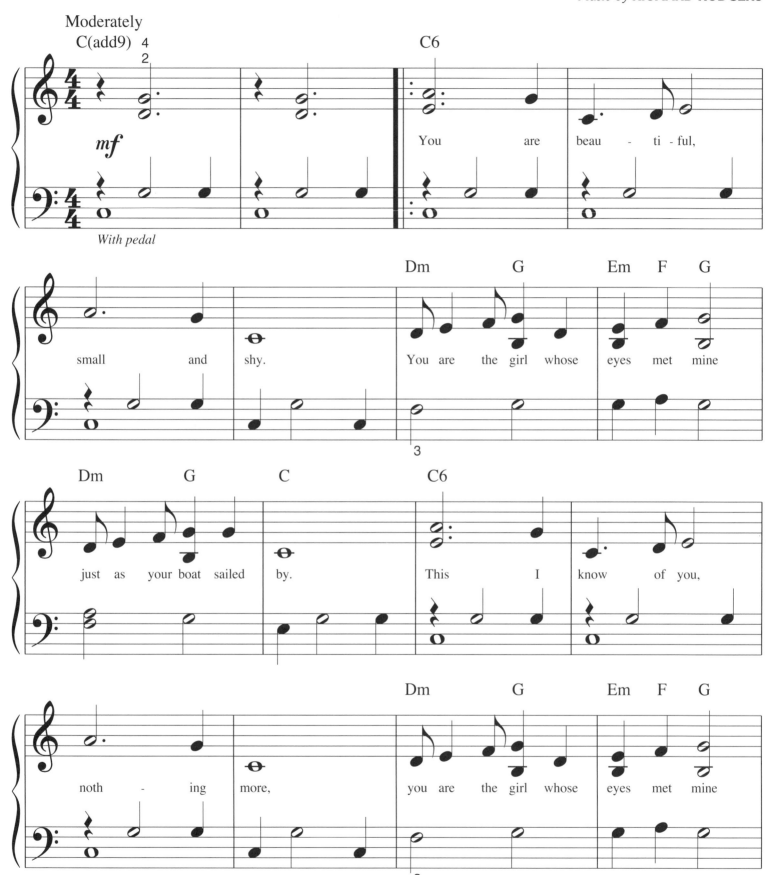

YOU'LL NEVER WALK ALONE

from CAROUSEL

Lyrics by OSCAR HAMMERSTEIN II
Music by RICHARD RODGERS

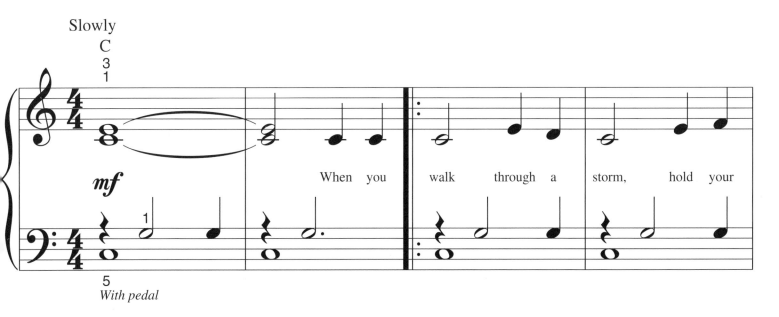

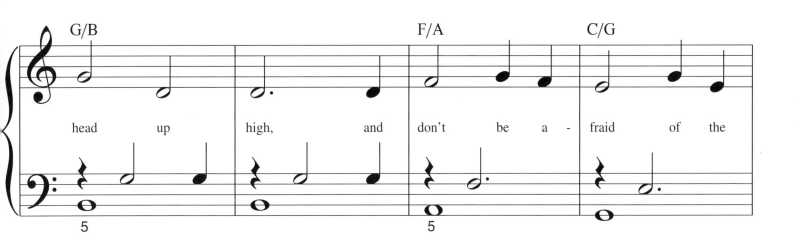

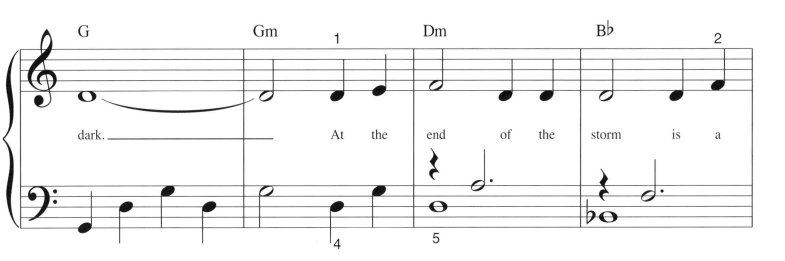

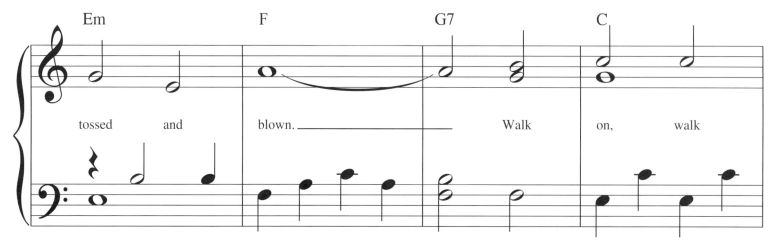

YOUNGER THAN SPRINGTIME
from SOUTH PACIFIC

Lyrics by OSCAR HAMMERSTEIN II
Music by RICHARD RODGERS